A Benjamin Blog and His Inquisitive Dog Guide

Italy

Anita Ganeri

heinemann raintree

© 2016 Heinemann-Raintree
an imprint of Capstone Global Library, LLC
Chicago, Illinois

To contact Capstone Global Library please phone 800-747-4992, or visit our website
www.capstonepub.com

Edited by Helen Cox Cannons
Designed by Philippa Jenkins and Tim Bond
Original illustrations © Capstone Global Library Limited 2015
Original map illustration by Oxford Designers and Illustrators
Ben and Barko Illustrated by Sernur ISIK
Picture research by Svetlana Zhurkin
Production by Helen McCreath
Originated by Capstone Global Library Limited

Library of Congress Cataloging-in-Publication Data
Ganeri, Anita, 1961-
  Italy / Anita Ganeri.
    pages cm.—(Country guides, with Benjamin Blog and his inquisitive dog)
  Includes bibliographical references and index.
  ISBN 978-1-4109-7995-7 (hb)—ISBN 978-1-4109-8001-4 (pb)—ISBN 978-1-4109-8012-0 (ebook) 1. Italy—Juvenile literature. I. Title.

DG417.G26 2015
945—dc23   2014043976

This book has been officially leveled by using the F&P Text Level Gradient™ Leveling System.

Acknowledgments
We would like to thank the following for permission to reproduce photographs: Alamy: CuboImages srl, 11, dbimages, 22; iStockphoto: guenterguni, 15; Newscom: Polaris/CPP/Osservatore Romano, 18, Robert Harding/Luca Tettoni, 20, Zuma Press/Pietro Crocchioni, 23; Shutterstock: Alexandra Lande, 9, Amy Nichole Harris, 26, BlueSkyImage, 21, Boerescu, 14, canadastock, cover, Claudio Zaccherini, 7, fayska, 4, gkuna, 24, Janis Smits, 8, Jean Morrison, 10, Luciano Mortula, 19, Mikadun, 27, 29, Noppasin, 28, Paolo Bona, 25, Serg Zastavkin, 6, S-F, 13, Stefano Carocci Photography, 12; SuperStock: age footstock, 17, Marka, 16.

Printed in the United States of America.
002713

Some words are shown in bold, **like this**. You can find out what they mean by looking in the glossary.

Contents

Welcome to Italy!. 4

The Story of Italy. 6

Volcanoes, Mountains, Lakes,
   and Islands 8

City Sights 12

Buongiorno!. 14

Buon Appetito!. 20

Opera and Soccer 22

From Chianti to the Catwalk. 24

And Finally... 26

Italy Fact File 28

Italy Quiz 29

Glossary 30

Find Out More 31

Index 32

Welcome to Italy!

Hello! My name is Benjamin Blog, and this is Barko Polo, my **inquisitive** dog. (He is named after the ancient explorer **Marco Polo**.) We have just returned from our latest adventure— exploring Italy. We put this book together from some of the blog posts we wrote along the way.

FRANCE
GERMANY
SLOVAKIA
SWITZERLAND — LIECHTENSTEIN
AUSTRIA
A L P S
HUNGARY
DOLOMITES
SLOVENIA
■ Milan
CROATIA
■ Turin Po Valley
I T A L Y
BOSNIA-HERZEGOVINA
Ligurian Sea
A P E N N I N E S
Adriatic Sea
■ Rome
■ Naples
SARDINIA
Tyrrhenian Sea
Mediterranean Sea
SICILY ▲ Mount Etna
Ionian Sea

BARKO'S BLOG-TASTIC ITALY FACTS

Italy is a country in Europe. It is shaped like a long, high-heeled boot. Italy has a very long coastline. On land, it is joined to France, Switzerland, Austria, and Slovenia in the north.

5

The Story of Italy

Posted by: Ben Blog | September 10 at 2:39 p.m.

The first stop on our tour was the mighty Colosseum in Rome. It was built by the ancient Romans in around 70–80 CE. The Romans flocked here to watch **gladiator** fights and wild beast shows—they loved it! It must have been an amazing sight.

BARKO'S BLOG-TASTIC ITALY FACTS
Italy is famous for its artists and painters, and Leonardo da Vinci (1452–1519) was one of the most talented. His statue stands outside the Uffizi Art Gallery in Florence.

Volcanoes, Mountains, Lakes, and Islands

Posted by: Ben Blog | October 28 at 8:44 a.m.

From Rome, we headed to the island of Sicily, just off the "toe" of Italy. I wanted to climb up Mount Etna. It is the highest volcano in Europe and it is still **active**, so I had to watch my step. If you don't like walking, you can take the train that runs around the volcano.

BARKO'S BLOG-TASTIC ITALY FACTS

The Apennines are a mountain range that runs for around 870 miles (1,400 kilometers), right down the middle of Italy. The highest peak is Corno Grande, at 9,554 feet (2,912 meters).

Next, we traveled to the other end of Italy to visit lovely Lake Garda in the north. It is the largest lake in Italy and a great place for vacation, any time of the year. In the summer, you can go sailing or windsurfing on the lake. In the winter, you can head for the ski slopes nearby.

BARKO'S BLOG-TASTIC ITALY FACTS

Many islands lie around the Italian coast. One of the biggest islands is Sardinia. The Monte Arcosu Oasis is a **nature reserve** there. It is home to more than 1,000 Sardinian red deer.

City Sights

Posted by: Ben Blog | December 22 at 4:33 p.m.

Today, it was back to Rome, the capital city of Italy. There are hundreds of Roman ruins to see, as well as lots of other sights. This is the Trevi Fountain. Legend says that if you throw a coin in the fountain, you will surely return to Rome one day. I'll give it a try...

BARKO'S BLOG-TASTIC ITALY FACTS

The city of Venice is built on a group of islands in a **lagoon**. The islands are linked by canals, and you have to get around by boat. The Grand Canal is the city's main "street."

Buongiorno!

Posted by: Ben Blog | February 4 at 10:01 a.m.

Most people in Italy speak Italian. *Buongiorno!* means "Good day!" Then you can ask *Come stai?*, which means "How are you?" You can say *Ciao!* to mean "Hello!" or to say "Goodbye!," but only if you know the person (or dog) you are talking to. *Ciao*, Barko!

BARKO'S BLOG-TASTIC ITALY FACTS

Family life is very important to people in Italy. Families like to spend time together. They enjoy meeting up for meals at home or in restaurants, especially on weekends.

From the ages of 6 to 11, Italian children go to a *scuola elementare* (elementary school). From ages 11 to 13, they go to middle school. After this, they have to choose to go to a school that specializes in **academic** subjects, or one that focuses on the arts, technical subjects, or languages.

BARKO'S BLOG-TASTIC ITALY FACTS

Many Italians live in or near cities, but some live in villages in the countryside. In the center of the village is the **piazza**, where people go to meet friends and celebrate special occasions.

It's Easter Day, and we're back in Rome for a very special event. The Pope is giving his Easter talk to a packed crowd in St. Peter's Square, here in Vatican City. The Pope is the head of the **Roman Catholic** Church. Most people in Italy are Roman Catholics.

BARKO'S BLOG-TASTIC ITALY FACTS

Every year, usually in February, a **carnival** takes place in Venice. People dress up in beautiful costumes decorated with gold, crystals, and feathers. Their masks are made from leather, clay, or glass.

Buon Appetito!

Posted by: Ben Blog | May 2 at 5:22 p.m.

After a busy day of sightseeing, we stopped off for something to eat. Italy is famous for yummy pasta and pizza. In a **pizzeria**, the pizzas are baked in a brick oven. I've ordered a margherita pizza, with tomatoes and cheese. I can't wait to dig in!

BARKO'S BLOG-TASTIC ITALY FACTS

Coffee is a very popular drink in Italy, but you need to know what to order. An espresso is a small cup of strong, black coffee. A cappuccino is a large cup of frothy, milky coffee.

Opera and Soccer

Posted by: Ben Blog | June 11 at 11:30 a.m.

Our next stop was the city of Milan. La Scala is probably the most famous **opera** house in the world. We're here to watch an opera. Opera is a type of musical play that began in Italy and spread around the world. Sshhh! The curtain is about to go up…

BARKO'S BLOG-TASTIC ITALY FACTS

Soccer is the most popular sport in Italy. Italians are crazy for soccer. The national team is called the Azzurri ("light blues"), after the color of its jerseys. *Forza, Azzurri!* (Go, Azzurri!)

From Chianti to the Catwalk

Italy is one of the world's biggest winemakers. These **vineyards** in Chianti grow grapes for making into wine that is famous around the world. Farmers in the Italian countryside also grow fruits, vegetables, nuts (such as almonds), and olives for making into olive oil.

And Finally...

Our trip is nearly over, but I couldn't leave Italy without visiting Pompeii. In 79 CE, Mount Vesuvius, a volcano near Naples, erupted and buried the town of Pompeii in ash. People were killed instantly. You can still see the ruins of the town today—it's a ghostly sight.

BARKO'S BLOG-TASTIC ITALY FACTS

The "Leaning Tower" of Pisa started to lean when it was being built in the 12th century. One side sank into the soil. **Engineers** have now made the tower safe, but it is still lopsided.

Italy Fact File

Area: 116,358 square miles
(301,336 square kilometers)

Population: 61,680,122 (2014)

Capital city: Rome

Other main cities: Milan, Naples, Turin

Language: Italian

Main religion: Christianity (**Roman Catholic**)

Highest mountain: Monte Bianco de Courmayeur
(15,577 feet/4,748 meters)

Longest river: Po (405 miles/628 kilometers)

Currency: Euro

Italy Quiz

Find out how much you know about Italy with our quick quiz.

1. How do you say "Good day" in Italian?
a) *Buon appetito*
b) *Buongiorno*
c) *Forza, Azzurri!*

2. Where is Mount Etna?
a) Sicily
b) Sardinia
c) Naples

3. What is a cappuccino?
a) a type of pizza
b) a type of wine
c) a type of coffee

4. Which city has canals instead of streets?
a) Venice
b) Rome
c) Milan

5. What is this?

Answers
1. b
2. a
3. c
4. a
5. Leaning Tower of Pisa

29

Glossary

academic relating to learning and study

active describes a volcano that is still erupting

carnival spectacular festival with music, dancing, and costumes

engineer person who designs or builds buildings or structures

gladiator Roman fighter

inquisitive interested in learning about the world

lagoon stretch of salt water cut off from the sea by a low sandbank or coral reef

Marco Polo explorer who lived from about 1254 to 1324. He traveled from Italy to China.

nature reserve land set aside for wildlife where it cannot be harmed

opera drama with music, singing, and acting

piazza large square in the middle of a town or village

pizzeria restaurant where pizzas are cooked

Roman Catholic Christian who belongs to the Roman Catholic Church

vineyard place where grape vines are grown

Find Out More

Books

Savery, Annabel. *Italy* (Been There!). Mankato, Minn.: Smart Apple Media, 2012.

Throp, Claire. *Italy* (Countries Around the World). Chicago: Heinemann Library, 2012.

Weil, Ann. *Italy in Our World* (Countries in Our World). Mankato, Minn.: Smart Apple Media, 2012.

Web sites

Facthound offers a safe, fun way to find Internet sites related to this book. All of the sites on Facthound have been researched by our staff.

Here's all you do:

Visit www.facthound.com

Type in this code: 9781410979957

Index

Apennines 9
artists and painters 7

carnivals 19, 30
cities 6, 7, 12, 13, 18, 19, 22, 28
coastline 5
coffee 21
Colosseum 6
Corno Grande 9
currency 28

Etna, Mount 8

farming 24
fashion 25
Florence 7
food 20–21

gladiators 6, 30
Grand Canal 13

islands 8, 11, 13

La Scala 22
Lake Garda 10
language 14, 28
Leaning Tower of Pisa 27
Leonardo da Vinci 7

map of Italy 5
Marco Polo 4, 30
Milan 22, 25, 28
mountains 9, 28

nature reserves 11, 30

opera 22, 30

piazzas 17, 30
pizzas 20
Pompeii 26
Pope 18
population 28

religion 18, 28
rivers 28
Roman Catholic Church 18, 30
Rome 6, 12, 18, 28

Sardinia 11
schools 16
Sicily 8
soccer 23
sports 10, 23

Trevi Fountain 12

Vatican City 18
Venice 13, 19
Vesuvius, Mount 26
villages 17
volcanoes 8, 26

wildlife 11
winemaking 24